Miming Happiness

Acknowledgments

Thanks are due to Peter Carpenter, Jane Draycott, David Morley and Susan Utting, to my tutors and mentors at RHUL, Andrew Motion and Jo Shapcott, and especially to Kate Long and Samantha Wynne-Rhydderch for their support and encouragement.

Versions of some of these poems were previously published in *The Interpreter's House*, *Magma*, *The North*, *PN Review*, *Seam*, *The SHOp*, *Smiths Knoll*, and *The Warwick Review*.

'In Little Black Dresses' was commissioned by Selfridges as part of their centenary celebrations.

'Offspring' appears in the paperback edition of *The Daughter Game* (Picador, 2010) by Kate Long.

'Two Mugs' was read on BBC Radio 3 by Ian McMillan and five poems, 'The Train Driver's View', 'Urmston Brickworks', 'Typewriter, Offices' and 'Exercise Books' were shortlisted for the inaugural MMU Poetry Prize 2008.

The Night Trotsky Came to Stay was shortlisted for the Best First Collection Prize 2008.

Miming Happiness
Allison McVety

Smith/Doorstop Books

Published 2010 by
Smith/Doorstop Books
The Poetry Business
Bank Street Arts
32-40 Bank Street
Sheffield S1 2DS
www.poetrybusiness.co.uk

Copyright © Allison McVety 2010
All Rights Reserved

ISBN 978-1-906613-14-3

Allison McVety hereby asserts her moral right to be identified as the author of this book.

British Library Cataloguing-in-Publication Data.
A catalogue record for this book is available from the British Library.

Typeset by Utter
Printed in Great Britain by the MPG Books Group, Bodmin and King's Lynn
Cover design by Utter
Cover image: The Train Driver's View © Jeanette McCulloch

Smith/Doorstop Books is a member of Inpress, www.inpressbooks.co.uk. Distributed by Central Books Ltd., 99 Wallis Road, London E9 5LN.

The Poetry Business gratefully acknowledges the help of Arts Council England.

CONTENTS

This Year's Skin

11 Extra Curricula
    i The Lesson
    ii Exercise Books
    iii Six Rows Back
    iv Modern British History According to Mr Flint
    v Experiment
    vi The Young Person's Guide to the Orchestra
17 Two Mugs
18 Town House, Tansley Drive
19 In the Year of Splitting Up
20 This Year's Skin
21 In Little Black Dresses
22 Night Shifts
23 Land's End to John O' Groats
24 Offices
25 Head Count
26 Offspring

And another thing

29 Syrup of Figs
30 Good in a Crisis
31 On the East Lancs Road
32 In the weeks after rationing
33 Whit Walks
34 Women at the Swimming Baths

35	What the Women Say
36	Pathology
37	Making a Show
38	Breath
39	Button Keepers
40	Typewriter

A Grip on the Land

43	In a Northern Town
44	Irwell
45	The Train Driver's View
46	Urmston Brickworks
47	Backyards
48	No Tick
49	After Darwin
50	Beginnings
51	Like Coastal Houses
52	Surfacing
53	Family Trees
54	Timbral Praxis
55	Liquid History
56	Ordnances
57	In the Reading Room at the British Library

For Alan

This Year's Skin

... but the rain is full of ghosts tonight ...

– *Edna St. Vincent Millay*

EXTRA CURRICULA

i The Lesson

We write to ourselves ten months on.
The friendless girls dream of prefects' badges.
Gill asks how you spell R.A.D.A. and Lucy asks
for more paper. David Essex features in most
and we all see Purdy hair as the answer.
What to ask for the future, even if it's in three terms' time,
is harder than the cut-and-come-again of Christmas.
Imagine a letter you'd written where all you wanted
was to kiss Mr Waters, as he packed up his notes.
So the dilemma was where to set the benchmark:
too high could break you, we knew that even then, but too low –
too low would put you in the gutter for life,
the kerb stones always out of reach, the stars
inching apart as you write.

ii Exercise Books

Kat's eyes are the colour of chemistry
and Frobisher house-points, but when Emily
says modern languages are purple, I see
papal robes and Mr Gregory's Redford tash.

Surely French is in the ruffles of plane trees
and Drake's maps? And how can red be geography,
when it's clearly in calculus, in the paisley
folds of further maths; in Scott's immortal dash?

Livingstone and English literature stream
through the atrium, find us laughing at a leaky
pen. Thirty years from Mrs Wadden's speech
impediment and she is still Anthony and Lycidas.

I cry for Joe Keller, for his sons; for the cabby,
for the poor horse, for Stevie on the street.
And not even Mallory's orange zest of history
can pull me from her daffodils in class.

iii Six Rows Back

Mme. took us to admire Alain Delon.
The afternoon was filter tipped; the usherette
against the wall in impossible heels, the strap
of the tray raw on her shoulders, the shift
of weight to the other foot. Six rows back
at the Odeon I don't remember how bored
she would have looked at the time or the face
of the man who leaned in for his ice-cream.
I don't remember when I stopped reading
the sub-titles, or when I bit my lip so hard it bled.

Delon and the woman stared out of the window,
the bed unmade. And neither spoke, exhaled
in short asides, smoke taking the place of words.
I remember the school bus home, an older girl
allowing the conductor to undo a button
on her blouse: the exclusion of laughter.
I remember the long walk from the stop,
my tongue opening the cut, tasting it over again.

iv Modern British History According to Mr Flint

In 1972 Wilfred Owen was not dead and rhomboids rolled across the rules of our books, laid waste to double-history. In the nine days of the general strike and a year after Britain went decimal we fed our families of four on 50p.

At the market we bought cabbage for broth, and the butcher compared the cost of offal with enough shin to flavour the week. At some stage, Arkwright invented the Industrial Revolution – derelict mills were dusted off, cranked into action. Factories

were powered by hot air and James Watt. The dyes from cottons and wools bruised the rivers and bloodied the canals. An assembly of men downed tools, schemes were raised, the Irish were fetched and the yeomanry drilled in St Peter's Field – a cavalry

charge Tennyson did not immortalise in verse. At the blackboard Mr Flint unspooled the afternoon, and at home-time poverty kept us company on the bus. We did our homework to the sounds of the modern world – *Panorama*, the 9 o'clock news on BBC.

v Experiment

When I go back to Chemistry
it's to Bunsens stretched the lengths
of oak benches, to steady
deflagration spoons of sulphur,
magnesium hissing in the flames.

Diligence, I think, what does diligence
get you in a room of quiet precision,
everything buttoned up as neat as lab coats,
our clever hands recording in unison,
as though life is like this:

theory, experiment, conclusion.
Behind us Alice is using a glass slide to condense
today's sun into fire. A jet
bombed from the tap hoses Lorraine squarely
between her shoulder blades,

just above her Playtex, as yet
unfumbled, hooks and eyes, though she goes on
writing up results until caught
twenty years from this lab,
in a third floor flat, with water tenders

racing to a hoax call. And here it is,
in the space between front and back of class,
the cause and effect of heat,
a vacuum, the catalyst of time.

vi The Young Person's Guide to the Orchestra

Sitting in the panelled hall for Wednesday's assembly,
to the right of Sharon Booth, the neck of a viola
loosely in my hand, it strikes me we don't know
each other despite the months of trekking up the road
for lessons, spending string money on Fruit Salads,
never practicing at home. We're twinned by negligence.

I know her bow arm only for the lies it tells to Mr Payne.
We keep our instruments in seconds and mute.
They're hostages we've played the game of holding
back with. They plot for the day when we move up
to firsts, when we're required to draw a clean note
through a mouth already set with petulance and spite.

For all I know, things are still the same today – Sharon busking
at the Hallé while, across town in Gatley, I mime happiness.

TWO MUGS

Corned beef chunks and tinned spaghetti
over a primus stove on the concrete floor of our
new home. The cistern's blocked, the power's off

and someone's pinched the door handles.
We have a mattress, one toothbrush and the two mugs
we fetched south with us in a banged-up wreck.

Tomorrow the removals van will bring the rest,
but tonight, you say, *it'll never be better than this.*

TOWN HOUSE, TANSLEY DRIVE

Up past the gasometer, the blueprints
and footings for Meadowhall, a little further on
from the substation, the launderette
and the old dear interrogating the street
in her winceyette, searching for the shelter,
asking no one in particular if they're Ernest.

Halfway up a lung-burst climb (and a bastard
to take in the ice) is our drive sloping away.
We spent Februarys digging out, digging in.
And if the road wasn't enough, there were two flights
to finish us off. Do you remember the wall-heaters
on each landing – just the whiff of a warm –

the one on the top floor where you stood night
after night, looking out over the cooling towers,
up the M1? And me, one flight down, asking
where you were going, where you had been.
Twenty years on and it's still me and the old dear
asking the questions. Asking, and asking again.

IN THE YEAR OF SPLITTING UP

Like the man who lived eleven days awake
we were always on a knife blade
of sleep. Afraid, in the slack space
of a blink it would be over. We portioned
the hours like watchmen, served out
our time on uncomfortable chairs.

These were savage nights as we avoided
thoughts of mattresses, sex. Our storm
honed its leading edge, our bones stung
with the effort of not touching,
wanting to unlip themselves from hooks
of skin, their voices, like the white light
we used to hear when we lay down together,
when we lay down, together, burning.

THIS YEAR'S SKIN

is hand delivered in a perforated signed-for crate
I've eased around the furniture. I'll leave it to settle

in my dressing room with the curtains drawn, a thermal lamp
and some mineral water in an atomiser spray.

Thinner than my last, more exotic than I've worn to date,
it will need a special kind of care, so I've bought a book.

Later, I'll try it with food, little and often, before
I think of handling it, let alone of putting it on.

They all flinch at first touch, as though body-heat could blister,
but I've a delicate hand for fine weaves and deniers

and a wardrobe filled with cast-offs. I've practised on rayon,
shot silk, I can darn heels and invisibly mend stretch marks.

We'll fuse together, this skin and me, our borders bonding,
shedding sequins – our tiny opal spangles – as we dance.

IN LITTLE BLACK DRESSES

You'll find them in the changing rooms,
shucking off familiar things, stepping out
of marriages and motherhood and down
to smalls, the known particulars of pleats
and folds until the years have slipped away
like underskirts and they are girls and girls
not wanting to be thin, or young, or tall,
or someone else, but just to have their due.
Not stitched-up in emperors' suits of clothes
but with new labels pressing at their necks,
in Selfridges they change. And pulled from rails,
the chance to wear their real lives for an hour
over lunch, to re-dress the short-term self
in LBDs, their cloth re-cut and spot-lit
in the cubicles of might-have-been,
clean lines now, in dresses that fit them well.

NIGHT SHIFTS

All through the early hours we push
our cages down the aisles of blank shelves,
freezers buzz at us like angry flies,
spotlights dip their hooded lids.

We map our routes by lino tiles and points-
of-sale, in parallel, yet out of phase,
with daylight lives. All around us
price guns rattle off their discount licks.

These years of dragging in the seasons
prematurely, as we do, with Xmas crackers,
BBQs, keep us always out of time;
we track the sun like shadows.

We work as satellites, companion stars –
elliptic constellations in revolving skies,
the earthly pull of best-befores and sell-bys,
of trucks reversing in the yard.

And as we clock off, detach ourselves,
so we race forward for that small hour
at the end of shift when we slip
into alignment with our children.

LAND'S END TO JOHN O' GROATS
A Virtual Walk

It's thirty-one steps to the lavatory says Kate, and with that we're off. The office is clotted with us, pedometered, all high heels and pencil skirts, though Stacey's in in Reeboks. Our waistbands clock each step, like a virtual finger on a well-being pulse. It's a 10K-a-day race with six weeks on the timer. Lifts are out of bounds but walking lunches are in. The transition from carpet to tiles and back is tough on the arches, but we pace ourselves for halls, vestibules, for staircases. Corridors stream and doorways clog like old arteries. Our dogs have never had it so good. Tracking our progress on *Google Earth*, we plot the route from Plymouth, on to Oxford, the climb to York. Blisters have started to boil. One man is going it alone, flag-bearer, front-runner, head down and forging on, a path-finder, a Hercules, shouldering the weight of his heart.

OFFICES

Through the glass blades there's another country,
its language bulky in our mouths, clumsy
and weighted with acronyms. Here, we hold
our laptops open while we walk as if
cradling scriptures, or babies, in the crooks
of our arms. Go north in the lift and there's
a shift in accent, dialects thicken
with money.
          And in July this is pierced
only by the melting slang of Anna,
selling ice creams, pen to pen, cool-bag brim-
ful of Magnums which we eat privately,
like sin. The room outside's stippled with ducks
and a man astride a lawn mower lays rolls
of Axminster on the off-chance we'll look up,
which we never do: the gospels speak
in tongues, our babies stir, and cry for us.

HEAD COUNT

Today we are reduced to the prime numbers
of budget cuts and contingent staff.
The chill of rumour is in the air, everyone
pulls their mortgages and overdrafts
about them, extra layers. Someone says
they'll wait to get the lattés in, we all laugh
too loudly, almost miss the soft red rain
of Claire's hair as she tilts her head to the left,
so close to Mark's they could be kissing,
and only the slants of their mouths have
something different, less tender to say.
It's about percentages, market share, the maths,
nothing remains to be decided – the door's
already turning, turning people out to grass.

OFFSPRING

Someday, all the children I didn't think to bear
will come to find me. Fleshed out
from egg and sperm they will bombard me
with questions I haven't learned to answer.

Why didn't you let me have a dog, they'll ask,
or puberty? The girls will demonstrate
the flounce they never got to wear
and the boys will brood like storms.

Hundreds of them, each a calendar-cross
apart, queuing up to say: *you are hopeless,
mother, we cannot talk to you.* And fathers

will get away scot-free, dodge the flak,
bugger off down to the garden shed,
to clean the tools they won't pass on.

And another thing

The houses are haunted
by white night-gowns.

— *Wallace Stevens*

SYRUP OF FIGS

And another thing about the dead is the way
they always turn up, uninvited, or butt in
to conversations about talcum powder
or the internal combustion engine, or soap.
Even now my uncle is edging into the frame.
It's as if being dead gives them the right
to dispense with formalities and good manners –
the same formalities and manners, I might add,
that they spoon-fed us along with the syrup
of figs and milk of magnesia (look how
my aunt sidles in at a mention of the blue bottle).
Why don't they just go away instead of
rubbing at us like tight shoes or the loose
thread of a hemline? Last week in Waitrose,
my mother had staked out the baking shelves
when I was looking for flour and my father,
hand on his heart, was checking the labels for salt.

GOOD IN A CRISIS

At the time, the big debates were over uprights
and cylinders, over hedges, over front loaders
in favour of twin tubs, and how wise
Mrs Hassall was to keep her old mangle back –
handy to have in a real emergency.

Mrs Carr was always good in a crisis,
and you could rely on Mrs Howarth at a pinch –
when the budgie got out, when Jack knocked
the eternity ring off the ledge and down the sink,
or the time Sandra's home-perm went wrong.

Then there was the question of whether
you could get as much in the boot of a Ford Anglia
as you could in a Mini Clubman, whether it was
Anglesey or Cleethorpes for next year,
and how to practise camping under the stairs.

Three minute warnings were for nothing more
than coming in, cleaning teeth, going to bed,
saying prayers. Parents everywhere said the telly
had gone on the blink, talked over it, loudly,
or changed the channel for no good reason.

But at least there was plenty of tinned stuff in,
candles, sugar, new valves for the radio.
Everyone hugged as though they were going away,
as though something big was brewing, as though
the mangle would be called for any second now.

ON THE EAST LANCS ROAD

We always stopped for motorbikes back then,
whether it was to offer a bit of stocking
or well-chewed gum for a leaky tank.
Triumphs and Norton Dominators ditched
in lay-bys in all weathers, waiting for some soul
with a bit of fuel to spare from the spare can.
Gauntlets and helmets set aside if the sun
was out – everyone on the great escape.

We were a long way from the sales rep with his
turned-back cuffs and hangered jacket, ploughing
the outside lane from one deadline to the next.
Mondays and Fridays full of them and hauliers
hugging the hard shoulder, shunting their loads
to small-town England. There, on the East Lancs,
men listened to twin cylinders: the rapid-fire
rattle of pistons banging down the exhaust.

Timing, they said. And there on Sundays, stretched
out on tarmac, they slipped a world away, to when
they stuffed potatoes up the pipe, or popped
distributor caps on panzerwagens to nick the rotor arm,
or, if all else failed, to put a round through the grill.
They knew how to slow time down, shift it, stop it
altogether. There, on the verges, they cleaned contacts,
adjusted sparks, got themselves back on the road.

IN THE WEEKS AFTER RATIONING

                              women
put a little distance between their bones
and their skins, got used to the weight
of plenty. They burned their ration books,
eased themselves out of their thinness.
As nothing changed, so they hid
themselves away in full view –
by the mantel and next to the clock –
where no one would think to look for them.

Mirrors watched the women, time hung
heavy at their wrists. Boredom stuffed
pockets like worn down stones:
what then was left but to drown
in this new hunger of theirs? And as larders
filled out, so women lost the knack
of joining queues, settled instead for seconds,
hoarded crumbs under brave faces,
Pan-Stik, their New Look skirts.

WHIT WALKS

Daz-white on a blue day and brand new
from the skin out, the girls walked in crepe-
soled sandals and freshly whitened pumps;
past *The Cornishman* and *The Cock of the North*,
the Legion, and the working men's clubs,
where low, low walls were beer gardens
for the Jacks-of-all dads and women who drank.

How many, spilling out of doors and out of dresses,
off their heels with gin and dragging hard on Players,
recognised a former self in all that glare, the two-three
promises of drums, the banners selling Jesus
to the faithful and wondered where the unspoiled went.

And every year's the same: veiled brides, churched,
paraded in a patch of sunlight, the tall shade
of Styal Women's Prison at their backs
and up ahead, past Newall Green and Sharston baths,
the darkening skies of somewhere else, somewhere
their mothers feared, and threatening rain
as along the wayside women watched them go.

WOMEN AT THE SWIMMING BATHS

They enter the pool in shocks of stuttered breath,
readjust their caps and elastic as if somebody
is watching them – their dads perhaps.

Quietly they begin their lengths of ups and downs
though it is not the water they are parting
but thirty years or so. Steadily, in row after row

of meticulous strokes and disciplined
by lanes, this is how they carve their mornings,
sieving the past with clean cupped hands.

WHAT THE WOMEN SAY

On the eve of her operation,
they all say it's not as bad
as it used to be. Back then,

women died by the thousands;
infection was rife, and the scars
ran the length of their lives.

Today it's better, they say,
each of them wrapping their loss
in arms too short to reach.

PATHOLOGY

On this stainless table the woman's chest
is opened to the day. Stripped
of internal walls it dares you
to look at the frame of what she was
when she was everything.
All the rooms and doors are gone,
but you can still see the treads
of her spine, visible, helical against the brick.
Look to where the floors were,
peel back the lining, the years of flock
and anaglypta, find not damp, not dry rot,
but scored before the plaster set,
            I was here.

MAKING A SHOW

My mother wore a nightdress under her shroud
in the way I had once worn a vest
to school under a chrisom of blouse.

Gauze over new-born breasts, a membrane
of cotton that covered the render, that covered
the clench of ribs that covered my heart. I imagine

these skins of ours slipping away, the coral chambers
suddenly close to the surface, neither of us
wanting to show too much.

BREATH

And just as we settle into the grooves
of our bed, so they come back to us
with an unfinished rage. Some shrink
from chalk silhouettes – as slugs
recoil from salt – rally, while others,
lagged in coats and scarves, chunner
the darkness away. Even the girl, emptied,
who once lay down like a rug
that had lost the thread of its own story,
revives, returns to visit us.
Millions of them crowd out our room,
watch us in our trenches of sleep,
hold mirrors to our lips.

BUTTON KEEPERS

On Sunday nights in winter
we bring them out in tins –
snipped from summer dresses, blazers,
from cardigans and cotton shirts.
They warm our hands
as we rub each other's palms
with a currency of wood and brass.
I like the well-worn best,
the set of satin ones my grandmother used
to lace her boots. And sometimes
I stitch my mum into the seams
of my own clothes, like spares,
just to feel her nagging at my hip.

TYPEWRITER

It stored up its letters like tinned sardines,
before Gothic and Comic, when we said
what we meant, let it rattle about,
a racket of how we felt at the time.
This was when words mattered
for the newness of them, not yet
worn in the company of others,
when concatenation and Haliborange
clattered like a child's feet in a mother's heels.
To type was to run through a wet ginnel,
shouts heavy in our mouths, to hear
the slap of our own names in the foot's
repeat. Secrets like fornication and cunnilingus
came next, pulled from the dictionary
and pressed to the page, lines slipped
into envelopes, stuffed back into books
and hoarded instead, read years later,
a hammer of sound as big as the silence in *when*,
the power of *no*. How we bared ourselves
on rigid keys, heard our days in the echo
of that emptied-out rib cage
of QWERTY.

A Grip on the Land

The trees are coming into leaf
Like something almost being said ...

    – Philip Larkin

IN A NORTHERN TOWN

The buildings put out their colour like washing;
wear their reds and yellows as a woman wears
lipstick to bring in the milk. Optimistic brick
and sandstone crowd the margins and docklands.

Black is ferried in on a river that rustles white
in the sun, is offloaded, block and tackled, carted
to yards. You'll catch it at windows; in the stoop
people put on their backs for coats; in the long

drawn-out chimneys. Tomorrow, it will come again,
bronchial, mechanical, and the mills, the factories
will put on a quick fix, a fresh coat of *Runaway Rose*,
step into the day, breathe out, breathe in, go on.

IRWELL

This plumping-up, this habitual fattening takes us unawares.
        We miss the hourly swell until the underbellies of bridges
                are upturned hulls pocketed with breath.

This purge re-asserts itself on land, we play brinkmanship
        with volume, with weight. Our lives are bagged against
                the surge, the relocation of the world's water.

This moment, more acute, with time spelt out in low creaks
        is a dirge to summer droughts. Our things, on the edge
                of change, prepare for flight, for new margins.

Doors won't keep us, so we make barges of ourselves, migrate –
        a saturation of peoples, crated up for journey, unhinged,
                flung wide as on the verge of living.

THE TRAIN DRIVER'S VIEW

Mostly, he gets the backsides of houses
flashed at him like drawerless drunken women.
No front room frill or bit of net, but a dressing
down of open yards and washing lines:

the off-white news that filters over fences.
And in winter, as he slows for points,
or InterCitys, under the scrutiny of 60 watts,
he spots a woman at the sink, up to her elbows

in a row she's had the night, the year before.
He thinks you can track the changes here,
in the trip along a passage from front door
geraniums to lean-to late-night fags.

All of life hanging in an outside lavatory,
hooked like squares of hand-cut newsprint,
filled with things you've never had, and fluttering
in the draught of people going places *fast*.

URMSTON BRICKWORKS

Not much to show for it now
but blasted brick and from the hill,
across the flats to Carrington,
the Shell refinery burns off its oil
late into the night and pylons
make a sampler of the sky,
cross-stitching power with steel.
There are starlings most mornings
toasting themselves on tensile thread
while underneath the brickworks
unpicks itself. Scree is netted,
like aida-cloth, against the slow
crumble, each fall stained red
as though we've pricked the past
and it has opened up and bled for us.

BACKYARDS

The houses lean in on each other, thin
as undertakers, shouldering their slates.
At night a man journeys the roof space,
his emptiness audible above the tellies.
He flicks through weddings and school reports
looking for a blank space to slip in to.
No one complains. In hallways debt rises
up the skirting boards and down the ginnel
the bogus queue to take their turn
at peeling Mrs Taylor from her pension.
Parents dangle over cots scrutinizing their luck,
while another tells his daughter's future
with a glass. Divorce brews in the silences
of a back room, in the way a woman counts
the links of her vows, in the way a man
cannot shape his love. The headboard
and walls throb with their grief. Outside,
a kicking starts: hate wears a uniform
of heavy boots and needle-painted skin.
Street lights look the other way. Work
occupies the skyline: water towers, the pen
and ink of cables. Didcot gears up for adverts.
Mrs Taylor's got the cushions off to look
for missing Edmund's watch and fob.
Thick with thieves and dealers, the back streets
huddle, close ranks against the coming rain.

NO TICK

no credit, no never-never,
nothing on the slate
or in the red, no Micawber,
no HP, nothing put by, no tab,
no ready-money knock,
no tapping mates,
no pop shop, nothing left
to hock or shift or chance,
no pound of flesh,
no sharks, no shiners, no good
hiding, no seeing tos,
the living daylight
saved, no working over,
no reckless bets to lose,
no brass knuckles,
no Glasgow kiss, no toss,
no turn, no jumping
at the bell, no hushed mouths
behind the door, no flogging
of best coats and wedding rings,
no lurking round the corner
for the all-clear call, no clink,
no workhouse, no pauper's end
some moonlit night,
no going to the wall, no flit
from Queer Street, no whoring,
no boom, no bust, no
no paddle, no creek,
no debtor's gaol, no bird,
no time, no tick – no change

AFTER DARWIN

    We stripped:
shrugged off accordion fins, our sliver
of mail, spat salt bilge, grew lungs, fingers,
an opposable thumb.
    When our knuckles
left the ground, we learned to punch
above our weight, found fire,
bronze, iron, words.
    We mapped stars,
turned shipbuilders, plotted worlds,
traded flesh. We dreamed in blueprints,
made towns and kings.
    Our thoughts
were sprockets and cogs; we built dams,
canals, mined new gods: coal, oil, silicon,
we chipped the planet.
    And on Sundays
when there was nothing left to do,
we took to rowing boats, with lures and bait,
spent afternoons fishing the food chain.

BEGINNINGS

Against the skin of a balloon a man
is learning to speak. Puckering her mouth
into soft farts, the therapist says, *b*, *b*,
asks if he can feel the aftershocks.
The air inside the balloon babbles on
in reverberated echoes of her, is mute for him.
He aims for *b-ed*, *b-aby*, *b-ooby-trap*,
pushing through syllables on a red globe
stretched as tight as the belly of a woman,
where his lips once billowed, buzzed
the dark meridian, where he'd played god
to taut skin, where he'd whispered the names
of their children, like winds through a biosphere,
rumour through a colony of bees.

LIKE COASTAL HOUSES

Just as this house loosens
its grip on the land, faints
into the sea, I too would like
to crumble away from nothing
solid enough to hold me.

Is this how people are –
shedding themselves like skin
or coastal houses, pumiced,
that soft pounding into the sift
of something else too numerous,
too infinitely small to count.

SURFACING

for Elaine

Clearly, on the slip-cover of the moon my sister
is learning to swim. She cleaves the ward's shade.

Her strokes cut a swathe through powdered water.
She has conquered, at last, her fear of drowning.

Her costume is the pastel blaze of memory, her
cap punctuates each turn, a cursor for movement.

She is sublime in her task, as though she were
skimming the lanes of her life in a Victorian pool.

Such determination, each kick, each palming of dust
to the long thin pace of the moon's breath.

I call to her in her mirage but on she swims, a shiver,
a shine, surfacing for air; slip-streaming the light.

FAMILY TREES
China

There are no aunts or brothers or sisters here;
we do not branch, we run on lines and wires
instead, a linear life, selfless and fierce.

Relieved of tributary roles, siblings, each
of us streaming like rain, drawn along vines
in the same direction. And in cold seasons

we freeze, together and separate, verticals;
like stalactites reaching in slow-drip time
for the touch of something filial, like earth.

TIMBRAL PRAXIS

And still, at five bells and, before the sun,
you can hear trees speak the old languages,
creaking out their stories of first crossings,
the effects of high seas on the uprooted.
In summer, this is lost in a swell of leaves
as though they wish to keep their mother
tongues from us.
                      Yet walk there through
autumn and the heights are tidal, blasted
by winds – the ocean beaching itself on shingle
and answered in the naked woods of winter
when birch, larch, beech ease out
their meagre words more freely, tumble,
lean one psalm against the next, branches
outstretched as though to catch their leeway.

LIQUID HISTORY

> *The Thames is liquid history*
>   – John Burns MP, 1929

A man pulls gubbins from the Thames, hears
their chalky mouths long before he sees them;
small things like bones and cup handles, chiming
in their estuary tongues of click and tap, click
and tap, or roofing tiles that have worked themselves
to smooth, to tokens of former highs, current lows.

Clay pipes hoo-hooing in their tussle with the drifts
and all those bottle stoppers, whose names
have crossed a billion lips a thousand times or more,
now lick the foreshore in an aftertaste of fizz:
Tizer, Helborne, Bulmers, Fremlin, Wilson, White.
They could be tube stops on a London line,

these fragments from the daily grind, daily ground
again, reclaimed from the dredge and drudgery
of years, blanched with salt and ditched like windfall
from pier heads, docks and public houses.
The lives this city lives: that double fermentation,
all of it dumped, collected, preserved in silt.

ORDNANCES
Ypres, 2008

We've fallen back. Again the whistle
signals a live round among what is mostly
tinder and baccy boxes, tin hats, the odd letter
welded to a jacket pocket (no jacket).
In the thick of it all, and newly drafted,
we unearth exhibits – sluice, number, label.

Controlled explosions, loud in the singular,
ricochet back and forth, a kind of echo
sonorous but dulled. We're six feet down,
shovelling war; blisters, moans about conditions
are not aired here among yet more boots,
adding to the growing piles of lefts and rights,
leather compacted, rotten with years, unknowable.
And some of them still occupied, like shells.

IN THE READING ROOM AT THE BRITISH LIBRARY

you can hear the sea. And in this noiseless place,
a pin drop from a milliner's grip some ninety years
away, or a wren caught in the eaves of a sudden thought.
There's a finger, sweat greasing its trigger at dawn
as it eases back to join the volley of twelve Enfields
in the yard, dust falling from the walls as we all
fall in time. A rage of sound exalted to stillness
and it carries down the decades. Even after-hours
the librarians whisper here, afraid to weigh their loss
or private joy against the din. As though one
misplaced word could creak like a nightingale
on a parquet floor, jar like a note in a symphony
of counted bars at rest, could make you miss the atom
cracking with the thunder of a goldcrest's heart.